DEW AND BROKEN GLASS

DEW AND BROKEN GLASS

PENNY DRYSDALE

RECENT
WORK
PRESS

Dew and Broken Glass
Recent Work Press
Canberra, Australia

Copyright © Penny Drysdale 2017

National Library of Australia
Cataloguing-in-Publication entry.

Drysdale, Penny
Dew and Broken Glass/ Penny Drysdale
ISBN: 9780995353831 (paperback)

Australian poetry
Poetry—21st century

All rights reserved. This book is copyright. Except for private study, research, criticism or reviews as permitted under the Copyright Act, no part of this book may be reproduced, stored in a retrieval system, or transmitted in any form by any means without prior written permission. Enquiries should be addressed to the publisher.

Cover image: Fran Whitty © 2017
Cover design: Recent Work Press
Set in Bembo 11pt

recentworkpress.com

for Akeyulerre
and Fran Whitty
without whom
I would still
be stone

Contents

newcomer	1
hot day in temporary accommodation	2
rock	4
traditional learning	6
sunday morning	7
edge	9
along the river	11
woman and ant	13
later on tonight	14
driven	16
skin	18
flesh and milk	20
bumble bee	22
little shadows	24
the light is not like buttermilk	29
bird	32
this wind	33
stick figure	36
somewhere	38
red river gum	39
sorry business	42
she quit for personal reasons	44
claypan	46
the trap	49
piles of small clothing	54
surrender	56
territory night	58
24 hour shop	61
visitor	64
little gifts	68
stones	71
a soft push	73

a song cycle of palinodes	75
fallen	79
smoking ceremony	84
big bed	88
two sisters	90
sing up the sun	91
Afterword	93

'Each day I measure myself.'
>Rod Moss
>*One Thousand Cuts*

'…there's no such thing as learning by yourself.'
>Margaret Kemarre Turner OAM
>*Iwenhe Tyerrtye: What it means to be an Aboriginal person*

newcomer

bark is separating
from that tree
        but clinging

skin is separating
from this body
        but clinging

the interior looks smooth
        but feels rough
it looks pink

        but it is yellow
        white
        afraid

hot day in temporary accommodation

dress hung over
an ironing board
straps dangling
a fan
keeps
turning

flowers on the couch
all flat
like a pattern
tired
of repeating
itself

a moth flies
into the lamp
smoke starts to rise
in light is heat
truth
usually burns

I lie on my back
old skin coming loose
gouging trenches in
a narrow margin
so this pen
will flow again

a sullied page
held up above me
like the sky
like a lid
and me below
too heavy to boil

rock

i

what I know is
people camp in river beds
care for children
place seeds in hollowed rock
grind them with a smooth stone
to powder
and the hollow grows slowly deeper
and something is cooked on the fire
that's how it was

ii

what I don't know is
how it feels
to have your land stolen
your law stolen
your culture stolen
your women stolen
your children stolen
and the sorry cuts score
this land

iii

and what I don't know is
how to begin
to fix such damage
ash pushed into scars so they will never
fade or lighten
poison tipped into so many mouths to
numb numb
numb

iv

and what I don't want to know
    to see
is my captain self as conqueror
sailing to new and distant shores
on a big ship a fleet
alighting with my books my supplies
my rum my prisoners
building towers
imposing words into that silent
open space
that is
not mine

traditional learning

for Margaret Kemarre Turner OAM

running | as if my life depends on it | past people outside the todd hotel | past people sitting on a bench in the sunshine | past people sitting on the grass selling paintings | I have | no time | to day | to stop | to speak to them | I have to get to the bookshop before five I need a copy of that book | what it means to be an Aboriginal person | something thick square weighty to hold on to | as I walk back up the mall | something with corners | new white pages | on which my eyes can rest

sunday morning

I have just spent the night
on this land with
this land
the sky spinning
or is it me spinning

I introduced myself
to the country
like the arrernte
but it doesn't
know me yet

there are so many things
that don't belong
collared dogs rustle
through buffel grass
mexican poppies push up

through sand they remind me
of holly little wreaths
of holly relics from a birth
in a different
hemisphere

I pull them out
we all pull them out
and being so young
they don't have much grip
on the earth

the more we pull
the more we find
young single roots
penetrating
a bed so old

river red gums watch over us
blunt old stumps
big families of leaves
and sunday morning passes
with this sacred tending

this way of saying thank you
this way of saying
I will stick around
I will care for you I will
I will call you in the morning

edge

      water
      towered
      by red rock
I have a choice
      whether
      to get in
      to swim
      between such
      powers as those
      two faces
      looking down on me
or to wait?
      so I stay in my plastic chair
      from china
      next to my friends
      getting hotter
      wondering why the ducks
      splashing in the reeds have
      all the freedom
      and what
      exactly it will take
      for me
to plunge in
      yet I know babies
      have been placed
      in woven baskets
      along a river
      and released
hoping to be found
      everything around
      is heating up

  before my eyes
  a piece of bark
  splits from a blistered trunk
  with one loud crack
  and drifts down to earth
  as if there has been
  no disturbance
there is a line
  on the water
  between shadow and sunlight
  shifting every minute
  and I want to be
  out of this chair
  on both sides at once
  swimming like a snake
  or rolling my prey
I see a limp rope dangling
  at the edge
  of this waterhole
  at the edge
  of this
  my own prison

along the river

come closer | newcomer | and see | dew | broken glass
nestled along the river | glistening | steam rising |
dew and broken glass | orange peel twisting
away from you | like a child afraid of a stranger |
a car battery with its teats exposed | an orange price tag lying
in the red dirt | as if this land has a price | a spider web as small

as a baby's fist | each loop bejewelled with dew | the jewels so small
and precious they will vanish long before the sun sits high | glass
broken | shining | a silver bladder sucked dry | discarded | lying
low | its pointy corners poking up like ears | a yellow tin of petrol | fallen | rising
fumes sucked dry | and six misshapen eyes set in plastic | diamond-strange |
once neatly binding cans of beer | till each was twisted

free | then emptied | scattered | green debris | now twisted
or just flattened to a bulldog face | humps of flannelette around small
fires | elders camping | elders resting | until strangers | no not strangers |
drive right at them | scatter them like birds limping | smoke rising | glass
bottles fallen all around | yet one long neck sticks out | a black man rising |
standing | upright in the river bed | he sees them | and he takes a bottle lying

by the road and throws it at the ute | and then he too is lying
where the bottle was | while five white men and twice as many boots twisting
back into the white ute | twist white ute through red sand | dust rising
round a snaking trail right through the river bed | past a small
toy pram tipped over | buckled | past the dew and broken glass |
past pink pants discarded | legs all twisted | past a blue leg strangely

broken off a plastic children's chair | what's wrong | a bird sings long | in a strange
red tongue | a mother paints a landscape empty of her son | his body lying |
there is panic | and all these plastic bags are white | ghosts flapping | glass
broken | dew drying | a white plastic spoon twisted |
a white milk bottle drained | a white balloon so small
deflated | still tied to a white cord frayed with fear | and fear rising

like a white fence paling | white ghosts | black shadows | rising
from this forked river | still diverging | we are strangers |
so much stolen | years of dying and denying | and all around small
bits of glass glisten with the truth | the violence | here along the river | lying
frayed strands of rope | short of hope | light and dark are twisted and yet twisting
away from each other | now a family holds a piece of glass |

see it glinting | all this dying | what is rising? | from the window glass
exploding | our hearts are tiny strangers beating | truth twists
us open like a chest | small jewels of water | broken glass | along a river bed lying

woman and ant

one shy ant
crawls
senses its way forward
pauses changes direction
forwards backwards
this way and that
up over a ridge
feeling its way through
a wound

one shy woman
towers
wants to tear off the bark
quick like a band aid
speed up this process
find something edible
easily digested
something to fill
the wound

later on tonight

there are flies circling
a police van
purrs up the mall
        a big cat
empty cage on its back
looking for someone to swallow
there will be white eyes inside her
later on tonight
        bared teeth

further up todd street
turbaned taxi drivers
will gather on the footpath
as they have for centuries
somewhere or other
        just not here
an argument will brew
their circle will tighten
later on

they will refuse to take home
that blackfella
he real drunk but he got a fifty
and a credit card in his hand
I bloody got the money
        he will shout
but his own mob on patrol
will take him home for free
        avoid the trouble
sis will lift his arm
pull it around her shoulders

and he will let her
        they know each other's people
she will steer him to the car
he will be weighed down
by injustice and grog
she will be weighed down
        by him

we'll take you home uncle
        she will say
I bloody got the money
        he will shout
holding up the fifty dollar note
credit card one inch from her face
        so she can get
a real good look
I want a taxi

in the car they will talk on
about people they both know
he will stretch his arms and legs right out
        close his eyes for just a moment
until he fingers that fifty in his pocket still
he draws his eyebrows together like a ridge
he feels the hard edges of the card he will
bend the ends together till
        they snap

driven

bare chest||skin tight over bone||over muscle||drum ready|| to beat||chest thumped his own fist||a hope in the pain||it will swell

rain||nailing down|| skin thin||as a bat he walks fast||driving nails||straight into air||his forehead||the hammer eyes fixed||on a face

past trees||fence||cars blocking his path||his path||to the cunt|| at the end||of the street ||he gunna||fucken kill||that cunt

around||rides a boy bike nervous||as if||by circling||as if||this circling||could somehow do somethin anyway||he just gunna||be there

and||another boy||lags
behind||bouncing slowly
a ball||as if resigned
to his fate||someone
to pick up||the pieces||
rain still||coming down

beside all this||us driving
||windows down||rain
coming in||us shouting
our help||but he won't||look
at us||won't stop nailing
won't turn||to get in

skin

skin of another
can look so soft			so warm
as the sun goes down
on the horizon			that you want
to possess it you think
the only way is to		wait until dark
get a little drunk
take a blunt stick or		a sharp stick
wood or metal
and tear the skin		slide it right in
your skin or mine?

if my skin is			torn
i will fear you
and i will do			what you say
to keep you happy
to keep my			skin and my
self intact

but it might be
your skin you			tear open
then i will be drawn
to you and			your passion:
all this for me?
i can help you heal		i hope
then you will possess me
all the long while i think	i am helping
you

and through this
gaping wound   we are drained
of dreams
our lives   will end
or the pain will continue
we want relief   i do
you do of course we do
but constant wounding   is contact
between skins
contact as we grip   either end of
the knife

flesh and milk

bark is coming off trees
like pieces of torn flesh

wind whips through
small october gatherings
tormenting every one of us

we stay drunk crazy busy
because it is easier
than seeing our reflection
in rock

we are dogs who rape
and tear intestines
from each other

we are the intestines
dragged across the ridge

we are fur dislodged
clumped on the side
of a mound

we are teeth
and swollen teats

we are wet ends
of pushy noses

we are puppies
and hard bones buried

we are the sound
of howling we are
long sad howling

and yes
we too
are milk

bumble bee

the beds are all outside
one long row
on the veranda

a little girl in a fairy dress
satin bodice
tulle skirt and wings

but her dress is not pink
it is the colours
of the aboriginal flag

she looks like a bumble bee
as she leaps from bed to bed
over each human bud still closed

and puppies chase after her
bounding
and landing

no movement beneath
but where the sheath of covers
is split

a tuft of wild hair
is not yet erumpent
the young bee busy

with her sticky fingers
bringing the garden
to life

little shadows

    annual art and film night, larapinta valley town camp

i

kids sit on a mat
watching films
on an outdoor screen

black and white adults
settle into
a crescent-shape
behind them

a human coat
against the night

ii

fire
in rusting drums
burns like scattered
candles

iii

the kids quieten
when their cousins come on
screen

making a big red cake
making their debut
this veranda
a cat walk

music blares
adults applaud
the models raise their chins
pout into the camera
for as long as they can hold it
then collapse at the waist
laughing

iv

little ones in front
are just as much
part of the show

they will not be left out

their silhouettes rising
and falling

shadow hands wave
and eclipse
any other image

heads pop up and down
bladed arms
arc back and forth
windscreen wipers

the symmetry of ears
jutting from a closely shorn head

a wisp of hair
wild

a ringlet standing apart

a lone fist
triumphant

v

old man appears on screen
extreme close up
deep pores
tough white and black bristles
thick as
quills

a boy's dark shape
rubs the screen
like he is rolling dough
soft palms across the old man's
scratchy beard

a tender bridge
between two ends
of life

vi

old man is talking about the land
about country
how important it is
to his people
the camera pulls back

pans across
landscape
red rock
spinifex
patterns
on canvas

a perfect backdrop
for little shadows
to rise

they soon tire
of age
of wisdom
of listening
of sitting still
when there could be action
when they could be
part of
it all

vii

a shadow swims
in front of the screen
freestyle

another bobs
excitement
at such potence

one of the smallest throws up sand
in front of the screen
across the other children

they shield themselves from
dry rain grit
suspended
in a single
beam of light

viii

children run through the light
chasing each other

they are this movie
this movement

it becomes harder
for the grown-ups
to hear the old man

over children's voices
rising

each higher than the last
a squeal
a victory
an injustice
someone keeping order
someone hurting

a single beam
a big screen

where little shadows can dance

the light is not like buttermilk

it is a relentless
interrogation

stretching from one horizon
to the other

people in the distance
contract into sticks

puddles dissolve into asphalt
before you reach them

light burns the napes
of our necks as we walk

flies sit dead
on each clothes-line peg

spinach cooks
still rooted in the earth

the light is not
like buttermilk

it has abandoned a car
it has killed someone

it has put someone else
in prison

the children
weren't restrained

the windows have collapsed
and light

picks through the rubble
for diamonds

old ladies
have haircut after haircut

men bear
neat scars

like the rungs of a ladder
there is nowhere to climb

light steals the colour
from chairs

paintings of old men
in cowboy hats are fading

the light is not buttermilk
it glares at me until

a soft baby shawl falls
pale pink pale blue

around my shoulders
around all of our shoulders

as we watch the sun plunge
its fist

into someone else's
world

bird

a small desperate gesture
four fingers pressed against thumb

this beak of a small bird
reaching

this beak of a small bird
ascending towards something

that can't quite
be grasped

once twice
each time withdrawn

collapsed on a lap
a flop

near but not near
enough

my arm the old lever
is afraid to let go of my hand

afraid of what it might grab hold of
afraid it might yet fly

this wind

i

it is the only thing we have
in common

this nephew
this son
this mother
this father

these candles we light
this wind
that blows them all out

ii

this water won't come won't
come
this desert

this wind
brings clouds
and takes them away

grass blowing
sand lifting
a body without edges

before us a tower with stairs
an aspiration to be higher

names engraved in
rock eroding

the sun pushes us under
desert oaks

those great mothers
standing
one limb broken

a fringe of hair
hanging over earth

sweeping it
bare

iii

it takes them
this wind

they want waves
deep blue
white froth
salt to sting
and liven their eyes

they are under this sky still
all those dunes between us

they might be calling to us
voices lost

but all we see is
hair blowing

thrashing their faces
thrashing all our faces

stick figure

she was painted
carefully on a path

a round face
a triangle frock

a pair of curls each side
upturned

she was looking down
towards her boots

eyebrows raised
in dismay

perhaps alarm
at what she saw

her mouth still smiling
there unmoved

and where her heart
would be a dry leaf sat

its edges curling
like a pout

its veins all yellowed
yet light enough

the breeze
could make it

rock
and when it moved

its shadow lunged
a monster vaulting

from her form
for she had never

had a shadow
being flat

and unadorned
and then the ants

began to draw
their figure eights

small infinities
like fish

as if her lines
did not exist

somewhere

she called me by mistake at 10.30
trying to get hold of her daughter
this new phone is all messed up
we had both had a few drinks
I was safely in my bed in my book
blinds drawn eyelids almost down
she was somewhere out there
somewhere—perhaps at home—where
anything could happen

red river gum

i

limbs have dropped
more than once
and the stumps
bear wounds lipped
swollen scarred

       here it happened

ii

she had a beautiful smile
she made me angry
she made us all angry
she wanted to speak
to the manager
she was feisty
full of potential
young so young
we didn't know her

       here she stood

iii

circle of flowers
    centre of sand
circle of women
    centre of sand

grains all born
    from abrasion
pushed by feet
    into tiny peaks
flowing as fine chains
    into hollows
we must not be silent

    we stood here silent

iv

till tired eyes turn
towards sound
this new-found warble
rising and falling
as if he is mouthing
a charm
and the mother says
shhhhh hoists him
high on her hip
rocks him to a rhythm
now hers
little boy join this circle
    the only baby
    the only boy
a boy named
safe place

    here she held him
    we all held him

v

balloons drift
loose ribbons
we place flowers
next to the others
white lilies red interiors
the tree grows up and out
of this bed of flowers
already dying
in sand

        old tree somehow
        rooted in sand

        rooted where we now stand

sorry business

the scream
of a coffee machine

scoffing hissing
pressure releasing

metal belting metal you
gritting against it

no soft furnishings
heels echo

you wrap yourself around
fine glassware

so brittle you could bite
a piece from it

women whispering
like freshly washed hair

men thick set silent
but at least they are not

shouting
all the pictures are framed

they always frame you
when you are dead

the music goes off
for no reason

you are left
to swallow

this
absence

she quit for personal reasons

there are patterns
everywhere
out here

dot dot dot
dash dash dash
dot dot dot

I don't want to lick my finger
sweep anyone's brow
in a single direction

I don't want my hair tied back
or my shoes blackened
each day anew

I don't want to
tap tap tap
email in email out

a pile of papers
with a pinnacle called
the minister

a pile of papers but none
that fold into a plane
with any real chance of flying

some fold into hats
an admiral
like napoleon

I don't want to rake sand
this way and that
so people form an orderly queue

I don't want to tell people how
to spend their money
or where to camp

I don't want to be one
of an army of ants
hauling a moth for metres then

devouring it
injustices will not be reduced
by me counting them

lining them up
numbering the paragraphs
I can only live

like a butterfly
each landing
a pause

an encounter
with something
new

claypan

i

giant finger print
pressed into desert

we walk around you
in circles
leash
hanging loose

every grain
temporary
untethered

queer ghosts of sand
rise on footless horses
glide across your surface

all moving
in the same direction

ii

you are patient
though you lose so much
day after day

till one day
you fill

you don't know where
the water comes from

or where it is going
but you remember

it has welled
before

iii

water like milk
legs bare
the sound
of lapping
is soothing

light glints at any
intrusion

a dog gallops towards me
a dog looks for something
beneath your surface

a family of ducks
rest in grass

grass combed
in one direction

as if there was
something maternal
in that wind stroking it

iv

old car decaying
in clay
I am surprised
by the beauty of something
once useful
now left behind

birds of prey wait
in the arms of a dead tree

then rise in the air

stretching brown wings
lined with scraps of moonlight
still lucent at midday

all this you hold
a shallow bowl

just for a moment

all this you must lose
forget and find
all over again

the trap

1 uneasy

this house is open | it is alive | day and night | the wooden grain along the window frame starts crawling up | becomes a gecko | bulging eyes | tongue flicking | insects thicken like a soup | the moths dive at the light | and other things with wings | a bat circles the room like the blade of a helicopter | sun up | I sweep the floor | the dirt grows legs and runs | I sweep it back | into a pile | it runs away again| again | again | a european wasp hovers like a halo right above my glass | daring me to drink | I spit a fly out of my mouth | it was hiding in a neck of beer | another fly is on the meat | under the net | how did it get | under the net? | on the window ledge more flies | dying slowly by the glass | on my legs mosquitoes lie | a row of ants streaming in | soldiers marching | single file | webs blowing | a veil | at a wedding | what a catch | see them stretch across the corners | catching all the light and other things with wings | spiders waiting | patient | but alert | mice peeping | in and out | of every crevice | very busy | and they run | and run| and slide | a dark streak | could be | imagined? | could be | a cockroach? | feelers feeling | could be | a feather | detached? | there was an old lady who swallowed a fly | I don't know why | I am an old lady who flinches at everything that moves

2 easy

this is the first day I've killed | anything | well anything with a heart hidden under skin like mine | I don't count the mosquito the fly the ant | they are numberless nameless endless | and it is | so easy | to spray | to slap | but then | is ease a reason | to kill | I have lured a mouse into a bucket of water with peanut butter | he is in there now | tiny | swimming | his front legs circling | powerful enough to turn a wheel | but the plastic sides are slippery | and I expect his death more quickly | not knowing mice can swim so well | but he is strong that one | he is in there now | and I am nowhere near that bucket | I sit at my desk writing of man's power | and salvation | in this heat | growing | delirious | with the circling | the circling | the circling of a little conscience but clearly | not enough | for I could save him | end it quickly | yet I wait | and wait | for him to die | there is a plague I say out loud | it's us or them | but that is always the reason | when people need | a reason | to kill

3 had it been easier

well he must be dead by now | I take a peek to find him swollen | lower in the water | legs circling so much slower | struggling now to keep his nose | above the surface | and on the surface | I am swollen | lower in my chair | thoughts are circling down like mad | I try to stop the thinking | and keep breathing | in the heat | I try to push him under | make it quicker | so much fairer | I find a round dish to push down | down inside the bucket | but he always finds the edge | the narrow gap | between the bucket and the dish | pushing up his little nose | I can feel him pushing | pushing | fighting for his life beneath a round dish | and on I go determined | to be fair | and in the end I kick the bucket | over | he tumbles free and wet and stunned | but | I would have killed him | had it been easier

4 making it easier

easier | make it easier | well guns make it easier | knives make it easier | not watching makes it easier | chemicals make it easier | planes make it easier | scientific experiments make it easier | a button makes it easier | a few friends make it easier | and a nation makes it easier | a commander makes it easier | adversity makes it easier | us or them | makes it easier | yes a reason makes it easier | a uniform makes it easier | and a van without a window makes it easier | little things are easier | things with no backbone are easier | and things without skin are easier | and things that are dangerous are easier | things with eight legs are easier | with six legs are easier | no legs are easiest | even four legs are easier | mice are (sometimes) easier | no voice is easier | a savage is easier | a broken heart is so much easier | a drunk is pretty easy | and a prisoner is easy | a released prisoner is | even | easier | terra nullius is (present tense) easier

5   nothing is easy

I lie back on my leather couch | because it is easier | and try to relinquish | this fight | in me | this impulse to control | to spray | to stomp | to trap | anything that enters | to break these webs apart | then I think | perhaps it is easier not to kill? | and I imagine myself lying in a field of grass | without barriers | without borders | eyes closed | resting peacefully | I imagine myself feeling | little feet walking over | my own skin | all different patterns | little feet | I do not strain to see which ones | something landing gently from above | wings brushing like a breath | over goose-bump flesh | a snake moving | ever so slowly | my body feeling him contracting and enlarging | as he moves | across my belly | oh so slowly | and in this state of natural trust | I do not flinch | he does not bite | and then thiz fly enterz my ear | zounding zomething like a chainzaw | I am slapping wild erratic | and the serpent he is gone | and I sit upright on my couch to find the one that I can blame | out of the corner of my eye I can see a streak of darkness | again | crossing the floor

piles of small clothing

the windowless
airless room

tomb has shelves
to the ceiling

piles of small clothes
all the way up

to the ceiling
nicely folded all this order

makes it darker
baby pink

baby blue
sizes marked

ascending like notes
on a piano

a few piles toppled
but the little clothes

still clinging
to each other

these tiny legs and arms
and necks I can't say why

remind me of bones
in a vault in cambodia

row after row of bones
crew filming

bodies
clothes

lying there
without each other

the sheer volume
of separation

the bending of tiny elbows
into narrow

hollow
sleeves

surrender

body burnt and surrendered
it could be mine
but it's only the body of a car

it too has been turned upside down
doors forced open
glass shattered

threads once connected
now bursts of crazed wire
loose ends but not quite freedom

boiling metal cascaded
like wax then hardened
into a new shape

whatever colour the car once was
has rusted to become
that exact same red

as desert
that same gritty texture
mottled dents and extrusions

recurring on its surface
a manual thrown clear
still full of instructions

pages swollen by rain
unable to be read
unable to be followed

desert you are undoing
the things we so carefully
manufactured

territory night

i

gunfire and
        missiles whistling

light thrown like rock
        above rooves

a black inland sea
        hanging over our heads

necks bend forward
        and back

colour born and quelled
        so quickly

the stars go pale

ii

light our wicks
        and run backwards

we love this frontier
        until someone loses an eye

sirens chase the danger
        it is way out in front

we peer over still
        smouldering rockets

want a better look
        at what went wrong

we want to know
        there is somebody

 out there to blame

iii

children wave and point
        their new toys

machine guns from
        the show

we pay to have the shit
        scared out of us

we pay for permission
        to scream

we pay for our cages
        to be turned upside down

meanwhile country music plays
        the ocean of love

guitar notes bending
            under the weight

of all this

iv

we make these beasts
        of light

ignite to jump and bark
            away at darkness

for what we cannot see
            expands by stealth

the sirens subside
            but in our beds

we lie rigid
            in you darkness

feel you swelling
            under our covers

under our lids

24 hour shop

it sits up there
on an expanse of asphalt
petrol bowsers

if there ever were any
long gone
but a roof still hangs over

this emptiness
underside strung
with fluorescent tubes

turned off
sunglasses sit on a stand
in the doorway

rotation scarcely
possible
coca cola has autographed

the bottom of each window
with the same dribbling
signature

bottles of coke repeat
in each frame
depicting an explosion

a craze of streamers discharged
from each dark
pressurised

neck
a white outside
fridge

is painted with the lonesome word
ice
snow dripping

off each
blue letter
the fridge leans forward

from the wall
as if trying
not to vomit

on its own shoes
a laundromat
rows of machines

doors like big round portals
escape hatches
no one opening them

no one sitting
at the rickety
picnic table

waiting
a metal fence marked
customer parking only

seven spaces
each fronted with its own concrete
ridge

the cars all absent now
have accelerated
more than once

into that fence
the row of dints line up
the fence

slumped backwards
like a line of boys against a wall
all socked in the stomach

winded
at exactly the same
moment

a police car drives past
although there is no need
unless it is dark

hot
heat pushing out of bare chests
colliding with more heat

heat
with nowhere else
to go

visitor

holding the door open
to let the visitors out
you push your way in

straight into my study
the one solitary place
where my mind is my own

you lie down
in the middle of the lino
as if this is your

final resting place
dust rises and falls
from your coat

a red powdered halo
descending
on a chessboard floor

you look at me
clouded eyes
that see very little

and I see you are old
hurt shaking
one long torn ear

and a patch still wet
on your back
from a fight or a car

you decline
fresh water
and you won't be lifted

or carried
you rest amongst the books
breathing

while we sit on the porch
breathing
wondering if we should call

the vet
but you emerge
lapping the yard

to make sure it is safe
we defrost you a steak
for a moment

you are young again
hungry
rubbing against us

as we rub our hands
against you
you sleep out there

at the foot
of an empty stretcher
at dawn

I offer you my hand and your
rough old tongue
coats my fingers

with a stickiness
I am not used to
I retreat to the shower

plan my day
with you there in it
wrap a towel

around my bare heart
around my pinkened
skin

blood close to the surface
I look about for you
now but the yard

the house empty
all that remains
is what you left

a still full bowl of water
a freezer bag shining
with blood of the dead

saliva of the living
a patch of dust
mapping my floor

back door propped open
fresh air
pushing in

and a warmth
once trapped
gushing out

little gifts

while women
come and go
he tends to me

he brings me
a spoon deep enough
for soup

        I think about the difficulty
        of carrying liquid through air
        giving and receiving

        something so fluid
        so difficult to grasp
        one person holding a spoon firmly

        while a young one
        or an old one
        sits more or less still

        liquid dribbling down
        onto some kind
        of towel

he brings me
utnerrenge
in a screw top jar

from a darkened room
in which
he is not allowed

I think about the stealth
and length of healing
about how

what you put into the jar
rather than what you take out
might be the medicine

how to loosen the lid
disturb and trample meat ants
how to dig deep enough

to find yams strung together
knowing what is worthwhile
to put inside how to keep it fresh

with open arms
he brings me
a plastic biro

in one hand
a blue lid
in the other

        I think about closing and opening
        biro and lid this endless tidal fascination
        putting it on taking it off

        amongst the piercing sewing spearing
        poking words down in their place
        on poems tombs forms

I am trying to learn
those words on the wall
I can't understand

all those words beyond walls
passed from person to person
a pipe a stick of fire

he is unsteady
on his feet
yet he brings me so much

the things he grasps
with chubby fingers
expand

as he hands
them over
the way a smile

expands
on one face
then another

stones

sit
separate
alone

nothing
between us
but air

over time
we push
against each other

resisting
eroding
in love

conflict
friendship
commerce

one of us grows hollow
one of us grows round
together we grind seed

add water
make paste
a dough

from the ashes
a bread
rises

this repetition
stone against
stone

a soft push

she is a slight stirring
in the trees

in the grass
she catches your attention

she is a way of sharing
words a thread of red seed

to wear
around your neck

she watches you
produce something bright

to admire
or a collar a noose

a memory
that old needle

uniting cloth puncturing skin
a red jewel swelling on the tip

of a finger
until the bead breaks

a print pressed on white paper
she is the shape of books spread

upon a table who says
a pile with such hard corners

must rise like a tower
when there are flowers

fans and shells to mimic
she is a soft push

air against skin
a current as you sit close

to a new friend
flicking through the pages

of a book
you were fond of

and haven't held
in such a long time

a song cycle of palinodes

> *Things will never change for Aboriginal people in this country unless whitefellas forgive yourselves for what you have done and open the doors to a shared sense of belonging. It is not up to us to forgive you...*
>
> Ali Cobby Eckermann

i

there is no way to forgive yourself

ii

just keep trying to forgive yourself

iii

something must die

something you were holding onto
something you were relying upon

the notion of standing up on a ridge all by yourself
the notion of leading an orchestra with a thin stick

the notion that you are separate
the notion that the things inside you will stay inside
that the things outside will never get in

iv

something must live

each morning
the urn must be turned on

two tea bags must hang together
in each tin cup
tea must be strong and thick
with milk

stew must be made in big pots

there must always be tails
fur singed black and scraped off
there must always be foil
to wrap around each tail
bury them under the coals

v

language must be spoken
word after word
sound threaded like beads

alakenhe

you must accept what you don't understand
what you will never understand

vi

forgiving yourself is a dissolution

you are an abandoned car
you are upside down
your doors are open
your windows smashed
you are rusting
you are burnt
you are crazy wire hair
bursting out of a tyre

vii

forgiving yourself is a weight
something heavy to carry

it is a candle
don't let it go out
even when it is windy
even when you have to carry it a long way

viii

anwernenhe urele arlwe-ileme

we do not gather around a fire
the fire is gathering us

ix

never
forgive
yourself

x

always
keep
trying
to forgive
yourself

fallen

i

out here we say what? to each other
more than any other
word

sorry-I-didn't-hear-you is
too much to repeat
every
time

rubbing each other's nose
in some deficit

when we are already
spent

one of us
back turned
walking ahead walking away
talking from the next
room

one making sound so barely

fans droning on
above us and ahead
they relentlessly
turn

we wonder if it's the desert or the
years

ii

there's an old cactus in our
driveway

he's been there a long time
longer than you and I

he is over four metres tall with perhaps
a hundred arms
sprawling up
from a centre
shared

some single some
forked

each arm ending abruptly without a hand
on the end

each arm ribbed with pores
and at each pore a crown
of spikes lie open
brutal

among the spikes
green spears grow like
thick asparagus
clenched
shut

in the
heat

waiting for conditions to
improve

iii

yesterday a third of him
came crashing
down

in our driveway
our entry our
exit

our vehicles
parked in the street until
we work out what to do
with a thing
of this
size

the severed arms still crisp inside
with woody flesh of white
that soon will brown and grey and
rot

the spikes remain

we cannot wrap our arms around
his fallen arms
to drag him
clear

we just stand and watch
his demise

all those tight spears
wasted

iv

you may think it not
much of a loss

but in the cool
of dawn those throngs
of spears remaining
will unfold
into a tissue-white flower
plush as a water lily
a broad face humming
with bees in the half
dark

bees nuzzling into inner yellow
threads

the pleasure won't
last long

the flowers
close and wither
dangle like
a blackened match
held too long
over a
candle

all these tiny dark
endings

smoking ceremony

i   traditional way

two rusted buckets
a row of holes
to let in the air

ladies make a bed
in the bottom
dry twigs and leaves

they add bright green
utnerrenge real strong
bush medicine

strike a match
a pillar of smoke rises
in one long stream

we people one by one
walk into the path
of the smoke

we scoop it over
our fronts
we turn

scoop it over
our backs as if we
are bathing in a river

opaque smoke
carries away
whatever is weighing

us down our spirits
now light enough
to rise

ii   televised way

flood lit stage
looms over country
a row of chairs

we wait for everyone
to be made-up we wait
there are strict

instructions he says
they can't get out of their chairs
they are all miked up

a panel well-powdered
four big cameras the cables
criss-cross the grass

she'll have to take
the smoke up there to them
amelia walks briskly

across stage
in the rush her stream
of smoke is torn

below renie and nidja
make smoke as they always have
but the panel stay in their chairs

this is television
the audience stay in their chairs
this is television

the smoke dissipates
it washes the weight
from no one

iii   out of shot

this smoke will be
the beginning
and the end of a show

that is not ours we take
the buckets out of shot
and the old lady says:

you've got to make them
walk through
the smoke

she scoops it over
her front she scoops
it over her back

a demonstration in the darkness
but the panel has begun
its conversation to camera

iv   old whispers

we walk to the cars
in the cold ladies sighing
old apere sighing

someone before us
has flung
a microphone into a tree

this weight on a chord swings
back and forth we reach to plug it in
old whispers are amplified

big bed

when I walk
this country
in the calm
before dawn
single threads
of web touch my
skin and stick
to my arms
and face and neck
trying to hold me
and I try not
to brush them off

now I am standing
in melbourne in a
marmoreal bathroom
before a mirror
that is not telling
me anything much
I see the old ladies
have come with me
creeping like smoke
through thick curtains
creeping through
the congestion
of a brain
that hasn't been
unpacked

they are amazed
at the size
of the bed
plenty of room
I hear them cry

two sisters

think of a claypan
always filled with hope

even when it is empty
especially

when it is empty
even with its skin baked dry

cracked and peeling
like old wallpaper

even when there is
nothing anymore

to hold down the sand
even when it is swept

into dark hungry shapes
even when they spin and twist

tearing up spitting out
stems once still

on the ground even here
there are two sisters

even here in all this
they stand

sing up the sun

old lady sings up the sun
then jokes with the sun
while we lay in our swags
at the end of the veranda

she speaks in arrernte and english
so we can understand
something of this crazy marriage
as she coaxes and cajoles him to rise

and I grow certain
if she doesn't sing
the sun will not rise
in this country

hush now she might sing
you up too

Afterword

As a newcomer to Alice Springs, I often heard a bird call—two distinct, piercing notes, the first higher and longer than the second. To my ears the bird was singing the question: 'whaaat's wrong?', 'whaaat's wrong?', 'whaaat's wrong?'

This refrain appeared in the first poem I wrote in Alice Springs ('along the river') and has punctuated my days since. I eventually learnt the call was made by a fledgling butcher bird.

To me the question 'what's wrong (in this place, and this nation)?' seemed no different to the question 'what's wrong (inside me)?' They are inseparable.

Indigenous poet Ali Cobby Eckermann said at an event in Alice Springs:

> *Things will never change for Aboriginal people in this country unless whitefellas forgive yourselves for what you have done and open the doors to a shared sense of belonging. It is not up to us to forgive you...*

How do we (how can we?) forgive ourselves for injustices that some of us haven't even acknowledged, that continue to this day? How does our shame shape our behaviour and our relationships (or lack thereof)? How do we put love ahead of fear in our relationships with each other? How can we be intimate without incessantly trying to change the other? How can we stop ourselves being complicit? How can we ever begin to belong?

These are both private questions for each person and matters of public policy. I always feel the weight of these questions in Central Australia. They affect the psyche of our nation.

One day I found myself sitting in the lounge room of the Akeyulerre Healing Centre. A two-year-old boy brought me small objects while I waited. I was immediately drawn to this place without realising how much the 'little gifts' offered to me here over the next five years—and the country itself—would dissolve my cage and recast my poetry.

Acknowledgements

I thank the poets whose workshops or guidance along the way have contributed to poems in this collection: Ali Cobby Eckermann, Deb Westbury, Shari Kocher, Mark Tredinnick, Leni Shilton, Deb Hall, Sue Fielding, Meg Mooney, Kimberley Zenith and Kerry Taylor. I particularly thank Jordie Albiston. The beginning and final stages of this work benefited from her sharp and wise editorial advice and her unfailing encouragement. Some of the work in this collection was developed at Varuna Writers' House and I thank Deb Westbury, Penny Gibson, Helen Thurloe, Kathryn Fry, Gillian Telford, Jansis O'Hanlon and Vera Costello. This collection would not be half of what it is without the ontopoetic discussions I shared with Craig San Roque over the past five years and my many conversations with Julie Reiger over a lifetime. Thanks to Shane Strange from Recent Work Press who was a delight to work with and made publishing a book seem easy. Thanks to Fran Whitty, Robyn Frances Higgins and Cara Kirkwood for all the Q&Ds, and to Robyn for her faith. To everyone I have met and learned from at the Akeyulerre Healing Centre—to all of you—I extend my deepest thanks.

'Territory night' won the NT Literary Awards Poetry Prize in 2015 and appeared in the anthology of finalists.

'Fallen' and 'river red gum' were finalists in the NT Literary Awards Poetry Prize in 2011 and 2012 respectively and appeared in the anthologies of finalists.

'This wind' was commissioned by The Red Room Poetry Company for *The Disappearing*.

'The trap' and 'somewhere' were published by Ptilotus Press in the online journal *Inland Sea*.

'A soft push' was published as 'Cafe poet' in the anthology *In the Pink*, compiled by Sue Fielding, 2012.

About the Author

Penny Drysdale grew up in Maryborough, Victoria. She studied psychology and law and has worked on social justice and cultural projects throughout her varied career. She moved from Melbourne to Alice Springs in 2010 where the poems in this collection were written. Penny currently works for the Akeyulerre Healing Centre established by Arrernte elders to practise and celebrate culture and ensure it is passed on to the next generations. Penny won the NT Literary Awards Poetry Prize in 2015 and was a finalist in 2011 and 2012. This is Penny's first collection of poetry.

2016 Editions

Pulse Prose Poetry Project
Incantations Subhash Jaireth
Transit Niloofar Fanaiyan
Gallery of Antique Art Paul Hetherington
Sentences from the Archive Jen Webb
River's Edge Owen Bullock

2017 Editions

A Song, the World to Come Miranda Lello
Members Only Melinda Smith and Caren Florance
the future: un-imagine Angela Gardner and Caren Florance
Cities: Ten Poets, Ten Cities Various
The Bulmer Murder Paul Munden
Dew and Broken Glass Penny Drysdale
Proof Maggie Shapley
Black Tulips Moya Pacey
Soap Charlotte Guest
Isolator Monica Carroll
Ikaros Paul Hetherington
Work & Play Owen Bullock

all titles available from
www.recentworkpress.com

www.ingramcontent.com/pod-product-compliance
Lightning Source LLC
Chambersburg PA
CBHW022228010526
44113CB00033B/724